AKBAR

AKBAR

The Magnificent King

Subhadra Sen Gupta

Revised Edition

RUPA

Published by
Rupa Publications India Pvt. Ltd. 2015
7/16, Ansari Road, Daryaganj
New Delhi 110002

Sales centres:
Allahabad Bengaluru Chennai
Hyderabad Jaipur Kathmandu
Kolkata Mumbai

ISBN: 978-81-291-3672-5

First impression 2015

10 9 8 7 6 5 4 3 2 1

Typeset by Ninestars Information Technologies Ltd, Chennai

Printed at : Aarvee Printers Pvt. Ltd. New Delhi

CONTENTS

FAMILY TREE OF THE MUGHALS

BABUR (1483–1530)

|

HUMAYUN (1508–1556) • Kamran
• Askari • Hindal

|

AKBAR (1542–1605) • Mirza Hakim

|

JAHANGIR / SALIM (1569–1627) • Murad
• Daniyal

|

Khusro • Parvez • SHAHJAHAN / KHURRAM
(1592–1666) • Shahriyar

|

Dara Shikoh • Shah Shuja • AURANGZEB
(1618–1707)) • Murad Baksh

CHAPTER ONE

YOUNG AKBAR

He was a headstrong and wilful young king. Few people looking at young Jalaluddin Mohammad Akbar would have believed that the boy would one day create one of the greatest empires of the world. For over two centuries after his long and successful reign, his dynasty would dazzle the world with their extravagant style and opulent majesty and they would be called the Great Mughals.

The story of the Mughals begins with Akbar's grandfather, Zahiruddin Babur who was born in 1483 in the royal family of Farghana, a kingdom high in the mountains of Central Asia in present day Uzbekistan. The kingdom may have been small but Babur had an imperial lineage. He was descended from two of the greatest conquerors Asia had ever seen—the Mongol Chenghiz Khan and the Persian Timur. As a matter of fact the word 'mughal' is the Persianised form of 'mongol'. However, Babur and his descendants preferred to claim descent from the cultured Timur rather then the nomad Chenghiz Khan and they called themselves 'Taimuriya' or Timurids.

From his boyhood Babur idolised Timur and his dream was to capture Timur's legendary capital city of Samarkand, with its splendid buildings and beautiful gardens. Babur did conquer Samarkand but he subsequently lost it to another claimant to the throne of Timur and in the process he even lost his own kingdom of Farghana. Finally, after many difficult years he managed to capture the city of Kabul and declared himself king. From Kabul, Babur's attention turned to India—a land whose wealth had tempted invaders for centuries.

Many conquerors including Timur had led raids into India, ransacking its temples and prosperous cities, and returning with camel trains laden with gold, silver and jewels. Babur gathered his forces for an invasion of India. The time seemed right. For about four centuries North India had been ruled by dynasties of sultans with their capital at Delhi. The sultan at that time Ibrahim Lodi, was a weak and unpopular king. The powerful Afghan nobility in the Delhi Sultanate was quite willing to

Timur handing the imperial crown to Babur.

help Babur against him. Babur first tested the waters by leading five small raids into the Lodi kingdom. In 1526, he marched into India with his whole army.

It was 20th April, 1526 when the armies of Ibrahim Lodi and Babur met in an open area near the town of Panipat. At first it did not look very favourable for the young adventurer. The Lodi army had massed one lakh soldiers and a thousand elephants stood like a swaying wall before them. Babur's army was a quarter the size of the Lodi forces. However, Babur had the mind of a great strategist and an army that had been hardened by constant battle in the mountains. Babur had a clear battle plan and he used his artillery with great imagination. He placed soldiers armed with matchlocks behind a barricade of wooden carts, flanked by his horsemen, and then instead of leading an attack he patiently waited.

Finally, his patience wearing thin, Ibrahim Lodi attacked and as his soldiers charged, they were met by gun-fire. Meanwhile Babur's cavalry wheeled behind them and attacked from the rear, trapping the Lodi army. The battle raged fiercely for hours but the Lodi army had no way of advancing or retreating. When Ibrahim Lodi was killed the army surrendered. Babur had won himself an Indian kingdom with the First Battle of Panipat and one day his grandson would return to the same battlefield to claim his inheritance.

Babur marched in triumph into Delhi. The treasury of the Lodis was at the Agra Fort, so he sent off his eldest son Humayun to capture Agra. In Agra, Humayun met the family of the Raja of Gwalior who had been killed at Panipat. Begging for his protection they offered him a magnificent diamond that Humayun then presented to his father. A delighted Babur wrote in his memoirs, the *Baburnama*, that it was worth 'two and a half day's food for the whole world'. This diamond was probably the famous Kohinoor.

Unlike Timur, Babur intended to stay in India. He established his capital at Agra and began the conquest of North India. His toughest battle was against the Rajput kings who had united under the leadership of the legendary warrior Rana Sangram Singh of Chittor. The two armies met at Khanua where the Rajputs fought fiercely but were defeated. In his journal, Babur comments rather cynically that the Rajputs knew how to fight but not how to win.

Then tragedy struck. In 1530, just four years after conquering Hindustan, Babur died at the age of forty-seven. He was succeeded by his son Humayun. Sadly what Babur had struggled so hard to achieve was nearly lost by his feckless son, who could win battles but was never very good at consolidating his victories. With a kingdom full of rebellious Afghan noblemen to be subdued, Humayun couldn't even control his three recalcitrant brothers, Kamran, Askari and Hindal.

Humayun decided to shift his capital from Agra to Delhi and began to build a fortress he called 'Din Panah'—the Asylum of Faith—on a hill beside the Jamuna river. However only the outer walls had been built when he had to march out to war. This new threat came from the most powerful of the Afghan noblemen, the Lodi governor of Bengal, Sher Khan. The armies of Humayun and Sher Khah met at Chausa near Varanasi and Humayun was defeated. He managed to escape by crossing the Ganga on the inflated skin bag of his personal water carrier. Sher Shan marched towards Delhi, so a reluctant Humayun had to gather his army to face him again. They met next at Kanauj in 1540 and the Mughals were defeated again. As Humayun retreated to Lahore, Sher Khan captured Delhi and crowned himself king with the title of Sher Shah Sur.

Celestial Sphere

Humayun's interest in astronomy led him to employ Shaikh Elahdad as his astrolabe-maker. His descendants, who included Ziya al-Din Muhammad, continued to make astrological instruments throughout the reigns of Akbar, Shah Jahan and Aurangzeb.

It looked like Babur's dream of an Indian kingdom was over. Humayun's brothers gleefully divided up the rest of the kingdom between themselves and they chased the hapless Humayun all across Punjab and Afghanistan. It was during these years of wandering that he arrived at a place called Umarkot in the Punjab where the Raja gave him shelter. Here, on 15th October 1542, his wife Hamida Bano Begum gave birth to his first son, who was named Jalaluddin Mohammad Akbar.

Humayun finally found support from Tahmasp, the Shah of Persia who agreed to finance an army for him. In exchange Humayun undertook to adopt the Shia faith and to capture Samarkand for the Shah. During his stay in Persia, Humayun was also forced to present the Shah with the last remaining jewel in his possession—the Kohinoor. The diamond would only come back into the Mughal treasury many years later during the reign of his great-grandson Shahjahan.

Then showing an uncharacteristic energy Humayun conquered Samarkand and finally his fortunes turned. He defeated his brother Kamran and entered Kabul in triumph to reclaim his Afghan territories. Meanwhile in India the Sur empire had collapsed after the death of Sher Shah's son. In 1555 Bairam Khan, Humayun's trusted general, defeated the Afghans and Humayun reclaimed his Indian territories. The Mughals once again occupied the fortress of Din Panah and Humayun's wife Hamida, his sister Gulbadan and his son Akbar now joined him in Delhi.

Humayun returned to Delhi as king but he ruled for a brief period. He was staying in the palaces that Sher Shah had built within the walls of Din Panah. A scholar who loved books, Humayun had a library in an octagonal building called Sher Mandal. One day in 1556 as he was coming down a steep flight of steps he heard the cry of the muezzin calling the faithful to prayer. As he hurried down, the edge of his long coat caught under his foot and he tumbled to his death.

When Humayun had his accident Akbar was travelling with Bairam Khan fighting rebels in the Punjab. When the news of Humayun's death reached them Bairam immediately crowned Akbar king. He was thirteen years old. The hurried coronation was held in a garden at a place called Kalanaur. Akbar wore a golden robe and a tiara and sat on a stone platform that was specially built for the occasion. Four centuries later, this platform still stands amidst wheat fields near Gurdaspur, in Punjab.

Akbar may have been crowned king but his situation was rather grim. Humayun had only managed to recapture Delhi and Agra from the Afghans. His hold on the kingdom was tenuous. The countryside seethed with rebellion. The greatest threat came from three Afghan

Babur supervising the laying out of the Garden of Fidelity. Akbar had at least five copies of his grandfather's memoirs, the Baburnama, *made by the royal studios, none of which have survived intact. This garden was one of many created by Bahur in his new empire.*

princes of the Sur family who were laying claims to the throne of Sher Shah and it was feared that they would unite against Akbar, who was too young to face them alone. Fortunately Humayun had chosen well when he had appointed Bairam Khan as Akbar's guardian. It was the wise guidance of this loyal old soldier that really saved the Mughal kingdom from collapsing for the second time.

Akbar's toughest opposition came not from an Afghan nobleman but from a Hindu commoner. His name was Hemchandra and people called him Hemu. He began life as a small time trader in Rewari and rose to become the chief minister of the Afghan claimant Adil Shah Sur. Hemu was a short, frail man who had never been a soldier but he was an excellent strategist and courageous general who rarely lost a battle. In 1556, while Akbar and Bairam were away in Punjab, Hemu captured Agra and Delhi. Abandoning his Afghan master, he declared himself king, taking on the title of Vikramaditya.

Akbar and Bairam Khan now had to take a hard decision. Their army was small and tired after years of fighting, while Hemu had won twenty battles in a row. He had a huge army and was already in possession of Delhi. Akbar still had his Afghan territories and many felt that he should retreat to Kabul, build a new army and come back to fight another day. The harder option was to face the enemy immediately. For the first time young Akbar showed the steel in his character. He decided to stay and fight.

Once again the fields of Panipat were the site of a crucial battle and again for the small Mughal army it looked like an unequal fight. Hemu had 50,000 Afghan and Rajput soldiers and 1500 elephants, while the Mughals had only 25,000 battle weary men and a few horses. On November 5, 1556, when the two armies met, it was a lucky accident that gave Akbar victory.

Seated on his famous fighting elephant, Hawai, Hemu led his army into battle. His initial attack was so fierce that it threw the Mughal soldiers into confusion. The two armies fought ferociously and it looked as if Hemu was winning. Just then an arrow hit Hemu in the eye and he slumped unconscious on his howdah. Thinking he was dead, his soldiers wavered and then fled the battlefield. Hemu was captured, brought before Akbar and Bairam Khan and beheaded. Akbar returned in triumph to Delhi. At fifteen he was finally the undisputed king of Hindustan.

Akbar may have become king but he was still a teenager and the day to day work of running a kingdom did not interest him. Bairam Khan continued as the regent. Tutors were employed for Akbar. However, the young king often preferred to go hunting or to tame wild elephants with a reckless, nearly suicidal courage.

The young king also enjoyed wandering incognito among his subjects. At times he put his life in danger. Once on a hunt, he wandered alone into a village and the suspicious villagers locked him in a cattle pen, from where he had to be rescued by his soldiers! On another occasion he went to see a fair at Bahraich and only managed to escape by some quick thinking. In

Babur slays a wild ass. From the manuscript of the Baburnama.

Akbar's own words as quoted by Abul Fazl, his court historian, 'suddenly some ruffians recognised me and said so to one another. When I became aware of this, I without the least delay or hesitation rolled my eyes and squinted and so made a wonderful change in my appearance'. And then he showed his friends the face he had made and Fazl comments with admirable restraint, 'In truth, it was a very strange performance'!

The result of this restless love of outdoor sports and adventure was that Akbar never really learnt to read and write properly. Later, when he discovered the pleasures of books he built a magnificent library in his capital city of Fatehpur Sikri but he relied on other people to read to him.

At court, trusted advisers read out the reports and petitions. Fortunately, Akbar had an extraordinary memory and seldom forgot what he heard.

The Mughals were an unusual royal family and took great pride in their scholarship. Akbar's grandfather Babur was a poet who also wrote his memoirs. His father Humayun gathered an extensive library. Even the Mughal women, such as Akbar's aunt Gulbadan Begum were scholars. Later Akbar's great grand daughter Jahanara would become a poet and philosopher. When the royal family travelled, their library followed on a train of camels. As a matter of fact, Akbar was not completely illiterate, there is one surviving childish scrawl which is believed to be his signature. He may have been a bit apologetic about his slow reading skills and bad, unformed handwriting but they were hardly essential for a medieval monarch who had to be a conquering warrior first.

What Akbar possessed was intelligence, courage, energy and fighting skills. A shrewd leader of men, he had the single-minded vision and ruthlessness needed to build an empire. When Akbar became king in 1556, the Mughal kingdom did not stretch beyond Delhi and Agra. The country was in a lawless state after years of chaos and there was very little money in the royal treasury. By the time he died, forty-nine years later, Akbar's kingdom stretched from Kabul in the north to the Godavari River in the south; and from Gujarat in the west to Bengal in the east and the royal treasury overflowed with riches.

It was an empire where there was peace, an efficient administration, flourishing trade and a beloved king. The

The widow of Bairam Khan and her infant son Abd al-Rahim being escorted to Ahmedabad in 1561. Her son rose to become one of the most influential members of the Mughal court.

stories of the fabulous wealth of the Mughal Empire had spread across continents and during the reign of Akbar's son Jahangir, Queen Elizabeth I of England would send an ambassador to the Mughal court begging for the rights to trade with India. Akbar's Hindustan was one of the greatest empires in the world.

CHAPTER TWO

THE EMPIRE BUILDER

During his first four years as king, Akbar remained an apprentice monarch and 'behind the veil' as Abul Fazl delicately described it. The real centre of power lay with the old general, Bairam Khan. As guardian and regent, he administered the kingdom and took all decisions of state. To his credit he did not use Akbar's inexperience to seize power for himself and Akbar's fragile kingdom survived because of his loyalty and experience.

Both Bairam and Akbar were strong willed men and a conflict was inevitable. His unchallenged power had made Bairam arrogant as he lived a luxurious life and treated the others at the court with disdain. He was a domineering man with a harsh temper and he had his own favourites among the nobility. As his unpopularity grew, even Akbar began to get impatient with his old adviser. Bairam did not allow Akbar any say in state matters and even the king's personal expenses had to be cleared by the regent. Akbar used to joke that the regent lived a grander life than he did. Bairam's arrogance reached such heights that once when he was ill, Akbar came to visit and the old man refused to meet him. Gradually a more organised opposition to Bairam Khan developed and Akbar did nothing to discourage it.

Surprisingly it began in the harem with the active encouragement of Akbar's formidable mother Hamida Bano and was led by a shrewd and ambitious woman named Maham Anaga. She was Akbar's foster mother and that position had given her both power and respect in the harem. Maham Anaga was very sure of her influence over Akbar and wanted her son Adham Khan to replace Bairam as the chief minister. Mother and son convinced Akbar that it was time he took over the reins of the government.

The dismissal of Bairam Khan was done in the usual subtle Mughal style, with a courteous firmness. Akbar left Bairam in Agra and went to Delhi, from where he sent a polite letter to the regent. The letter said that Bairam had been working so hard he deserved a holiday and should go on a pilgrimage to Mecca and that Akbar would bear the expenses of the journey. Bairam could have rebelled

but to his credit he obeyed the order and left Agra. Maham Anaga then made the mistake of sending the army after him to make sure he really was going. This was too insulting for the old man and deeply hurt and angered, he turned back to fight Akbar's men. Bairam lost and was captured and brought to court but by then Akbar had realised his mistake. The two men had fought many battles together and he knew too well just how much he owed this man. Akbar apologised for

Akbar hunting.

his rash action and they were reconciled. Akbar treated his mentor with respect and honour and Bairam once again left for Mecca. However, he never made it to his destination as he was assassinated in Gujarat by an Afghan soldier who bore him a personal grudge.

Now Maham Anaga and her son were supreme in the Mughal court. They obviously believed that like Bairam Khan had done before, they could control young Akbar and rule in his name. What they failed to realise was that Akbar was no longer a boy.

Akbar's adventures on his elephant, Hawai, from the Akbarnama, *c. 1590.*

At eighteen he had a mind of his own and was not willing to be influenced by anyone. Also Adham Khan was both over ambitious and arrogant and as he was foolish enough to defy Akbar, he quickly angered the king. The trouble began when Adham conquered Malwa and tried to keep back some of the captured treasures and a furious Akbar arrived at Mandu to discipline him. He only forgave Adham at Maham Anaga's request.

Sadly Adham Khan refused to change. Akbar had appointed Atkah Khan as his chief minister and this had greatly displeased Adham, who had wanted the position for himself. One day Atkah Khan was at work in his office that was located next to Akbar's private chambers. Adham and his men forced their way in, stabbed Atkah to death and then tried to enter the king's bedroom. Hearing the loud altercation between Adham and the sentries who were blocking his way, Akbar emerged from his bedroom to confront a band of armed and excited men. He was alone and unarmed but the power of his personality was so great that no one had the courage to attack him. In a rage Akbar punched Adham Khan so hard that he fell unconscious.

Then showing no mercy the king ordered that his foster brother should be thrown off the walls of the fort. Adham Khan did not die the first time and he was thrown down again. Then Akbar went into the harem to inform

Maham Anaga of his actions. She quietly accepted his decision and died soon after. Maham Anaga's rule had lasted only for eighteen months. Throughout his reign, Akbar was often willing to forgive and reconcile with people who acted against him but he did not allow anyone to question his authority and his royal anger was truly merciless. At nineteen Akbar was now in complete control and soon he began to act with great statesmanship and vigour.

In many ways he was very different from the earlier Muslim rulers of India. By the time the Mughals came to power, North India had been ruled by Muslim sultans for four centuries. There was a great social divide between the ruling Muslim nobility that was made up mainly of Afghans, Persians and Turks and the subjects who were Hindus. The sultans treated their Hindu subjects with distrust and the feeling was returned in full measure. Hindus had to pay a religious tax like jiziya, they could not rise to high posts in the government or in the army and no Hindu could become a member of the nobility. Some sultans took pride in being defenders of the Muslim faith, destroying temples, burning holy books and not allowing Hindus to practise their religion freely. For the common people of India the sultans remained foreigners and occupying conquerors and were never accepted as kings.

Akbar was shrewd enough to realise that if he wanted to rule in peace he had to gain the loyalty of all his subjects. The challenge was to transform himself from a hated conqueror to a popular king and that meant he had to be accepted by the Hindus. In medieval times, when religious bigotry was the accepted norm, a deliberate policy of religious toleration was an extraordinary decision. It was the result of both Akbar's ambitions and his unusual character. His decision may have been a pragmatic one but he was also genuinely tolerant and open minded by nature. As the historian Haidar wrote, he was 'the child of a Sunni father and a Shia mother born in Hindustan in the land of Sufism at the house of a Hindu'. In many ways he was a true Indian king.

Akbar's first revolutionary decision was taken at the age of twenty, when he decided to take a Hindu wife. This was not in itself very unusual as such royal alliances had taken place before. But the Hindu princesses marrying sultans were forced to convert to Islam. Akbar allowed his queens to remain Hindus and practise their religion freely and they were given separate palaces, their own temples and kitchens. Then he appointed Hindus in high posts in the government and Hindu kings led the army and were given titles as noblemen. In Akbar's government you rose according to your ability and this immediately created an army and civil service that was deeply loyal to their king.

Akbar always understood the power of the right gesture. For instance, when he abolished the hated jiziya tax and a tax on Hindu pilgrims, this immediately sent the message to all his subjects that in the eyes of the king Hindus and Muslims were equals. Also he was genuinely curious about other religions and would often hold long discussions on philosophy and metaphysics with the priests and thinkers of different faiths. Hindu festivals were celebrated in court with Akbar joining in enthusiastically in Holi and Diwali and one of the grandest celebrations was for the Parsi Nauroz.

For his first Hindu marriage Akbar chose the royal family of Amber (modern Jaipur). The Amber king Bharmal met Akbar when he was on a pilgrimage to Ajmer and offered his daughter in marriage and the king accepted.

Thus began the highly successful Mughal-Amber alliance with Bharman, his son Bhagwan Das and grandson Man Singh all welcomed into the royal court with many honours. The Akbar married princesses from other Hindu kingdoms like Jodhpur, Jaisalmer and Bikaner.

Akbar had very good reasons for choosing these Hindu princesses as he wanted the Rajputs as allies not enemies. They were legendary warriors and as none of the Rajput kings had acknowledge Akbar as their king they could become a source of unrest and rebellion. With the Rajputs as allies he got good generals and soldiers for his army and efficient ministers for his administration. And the Rajput nobility acted as a balance to the troublesome Uzbegs in the royal court. Rajputana was also strategically important as it was on the route to the ports of Gujarat and the road to the Deccan.

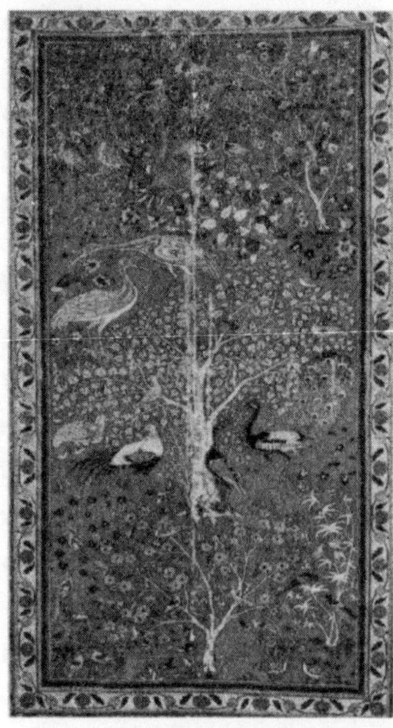

Landscape carpet, Mughal, late 16th century.

The Rajputs gained too from an alliance with the Mughals. Akbar left them free to rule their kingdoms and they did not have to live in fear of a Mughal attack. He treated them with great generosity, Man Singh was honoured with the feudal mansabdari of 7000 horse, the highest after the royal princes. Raja Todar Mal was appointed the revenue minister, Raja Birbal, was not just an adviser he was one of Akbar's closest friends. Later Mughal kings would continue this tradition and after a while no one questioned the presence of Hindus in the civil service and army. Both his son Jahangir and grandson Shahjahan, were born of Hindu queens and even Aurangzeb, who had an ambivalent relationship with Hindus, had a Hindu general fighting Shivaji.

Akbar was a true imperialist, single minded in his policy of conquest, with an insatiable hunger for land. Most of his life was spent on military expeditions and he led his last expedition to the Deccan when he was close to sixty. As a general he was a brilliant and inventive strategist like his grandfather Babur and a ruthless warrior who fought to win and never lost a battle. As his historian Abul Fazl quotes him as saying, 'a monarch should be ever intent on conquest, otherwise his neighbours rise in arms against him'. Akbar was magnanimous once his power was acknowledged but he was merciless with those who defied him.

Within a decade, Akbar controlled a vast empire and had acquired immense wealth that made the dynasty one of the richest in the world. Once a kingdom had been conquered, at times Akbar put his own governor there, who collected taxes, supervised the administration and maintained law and order. But in cases of kingdoms that were very far away from his capital at Agra, the local king was allowed to continue in power as long as he acknowledged the supremacy of Akbar and regularly sent money, jewels, even horses, elephants and slaves as tribute. As vassals they knew that the slightest sign of non-cooperation would bring the Mughal army marching into their borders.

Akbar only went to war after all other options had been exhausted. The annexation of a kingdom would begin with Akbar sending an ambassador with a very polite request that the king accept Akbar as his overlord and if he refused, Akbar would declare war. Medieval wars were leisurely affairs, lasting for months, even years. The two sides would begin to gather their armies and the king would move his men into a fortress and wait for the Mughal attack. The medieval army was a huge machine that travelled slowly and by the time of Aurangzeb an army on the move would stretch for two kilometers down a road. An army camp was like a small town—a sea of tents, stables, kitchens, bazaars and people. There was little, chance of a surprise attack, people knew for weeks about an invasion.

So Akbar devised new ways to invade and one of them was using the excuse of going hunting. He would venture out with a whole army playing the role of beaters and move right up to the border and then surprise the enemy. At other times he would leave his artillery and foot soldiers behind and just attack with his cavalry. Moving with a small contingent on swift horses and camels, riding day and night at great speed and arriving at the enemy's doorstep before they were ready for battle. On one expedition to Gujarat he rode on camels and covered a distance of 800 kilometres in just eleven days. He always led from the front and would fight with a ferocious courage, often putting his own life in danger. In this way he conquered states that had refused to ally with him like Malwa, Chittor, Bengal and Gujarat.

One of Akbar's greatest battles was with the one Rajput clan that stubbornly remained independent—the Sisodias of Mewar. The Mewar Ranas ruled from their legendary fortress of Chittor and were considered the leaders of the Rajput *rajas*. Rana Sangram Singh had fought Babur at Khanua. The present king, Rana Udai Singh refused to give a daughter in marriage or attend the royal court as a vassal. Akbar was not going to accept the rejection quietly and a battle was inevitable. The battle for Chittor is a saga of great bravery and terrible tragedy. Udai Singh was reviled for his role but his son Pratap became a hero and tales of his exploits are still sung by the bards of Rajasthan.

In September 1567, when Akbar arrived to surround the Chittor fortress, Udai Singh had already fled leaving behind 8000 Rajput warriors under his general Jaimal. Many historians have called him a coward but his actions may have saved the Mewar kingdom. He made sure the fortress could resist a siege for months as it was stocked with ample food and arms. Then he shifted his capital to a new city that he built beside a lake and called Udaipur. Now even if Akbar captured the Chittor Fort he could not claim to have defeated the Rana and taken the capital of Mewar.

Chittor was a formidable fortress. It stood on an immense rock rising steeply from a barren countryside and its high walls made it virtually impregnable. The Mughal soldiers could not climb the steep hill to attack as the Rajput musketeers could easily pick them out from behind the great walls. So the Mughal cannons were used to try to breach the walls and when a part of the wall broke, the Rajputs would repair it during the night. Then bad luck struck one night, when Jaimal came to oversee the repairs at one of these breaches and was killed by a stray bullet. Abul

Spoon:

Gold, engraved and set with rubies, emeralds and diamonds. Mughal, late 16th or early 17th century.

Fazl loyally claims that it was fired by Akbar himself.

The Rajputs did not believe in surrender, they chose to die fighting and the women died with them. The new leader of the Rajputs was a teenager named Patta who continued to fight with great courage but as the siege continued, defeat became inevitable. The men prepared to charge out on their last battle, as the women killed themselves by jumping into the funeral pyre in the tradition of Jauhar. It was 'the last awful sacrifice which Rajput despair offers to honour and the gods' Below the hill, Akbar looked up to see the spiralling smoke behind the fortress walls and his Rajput generals recognised the ominous signs of jauhar. They warned Akbar that the final attack was about to follow. In the last battle all Patta's men died and then the Mughal army entered Chittor, destroyed its palaces and massacred the people. The massacre at Chittor was one of the darkest acts of Akbar's rule and the ruined fortress was abandoned forever.

Dagger:

Steel with traces of gilding. Mughal, c.1600.

Akbar conquered Chittor but the spirit of Mewar could not be crushed. Udai Singh died in 1572 and was succeeded by his son Rana Pratap. Akbar tried once again to build an alliance with him. He sent three missions, one led by Todar Mal but the defiant Pratap refused to bow to the might of the Mughals. War was inevitable and the two armies met at Haldighati on 18th June 1576 and even though the Rajputs fought with fierce courage their army was too small compared to the Mughal might. Pratap was wounded but managed to retreat into the hills where he could not be followed. Helped by tribal Bhil warriors, he continued to wage a guerilla war from the hills of Mewar. Over the years he regained much of his kingdom and he never bowed to the Mughals.

By the time Akbar was in his mid twenties, he had conquered most of North India and some of the southern kingdoms had become his allies. There was peace in his kingdom and the Mughal treasury overflowed with gold and jewels. Within the first ten years of his reign he had become a supreme monarch. Now Akbar the empire builder began to transform himself into Akbar the king.

CHAPTER THREE

THE KING

In 1568, Akbar was twenty six and the monarch of an Indian Empire. His kingdom covered most of north India from Kabul in the west to Bengal in the east and most of the rulers of neighbouring kingdoms acknowledged his sovereignty. There was peace in his kingdom and few dared to rise in rebellion against him. Trade was growing and the royal treasury was also filling up nicely with tribute and revenue. In spite of it all, Akbar had little peace as he had no son who could inherit this kingdom. For a diehard imperialist like him this was a devastating disappointment.

In spite of a harem filled with queens and concubines, none of Akbar's male children had survived. He was a worried man and being deeply religious he now turned to god. He was already attracted to Sufi philosophy, often meeting pirs and visiting the shrine of the Sufi saint Khwaja Sheikh Muinuddin Chishti at Ajmer in Rajasthan. Now he heard of a sufi recluse who lived in a shack on top of a hill on the outskirts of Agra. Sheikh Salim Chishti was a follower of the same Chishtiya order as Muinuddin and he lived in a place called Sikri. Akbar went to see the saint to seek guidance and to confide in him his greatest sorrow.

Salim Chishti assured Akbar that not only would he have an heir to inherit the throne, he would have three sons who would live to adulthood. Within a few

Tomb of Sheikh Salim Chishti, Fatehpur Sikri.

months, to his delight Akbar heard that one of his Hindu queens, the princess of Amber was going to have a child. Interestingly, though popular tradition calls this princess Jodh Bai, none of the chronicles of the time, not even Abul Fazl, actually give her name. They always refer to her either as the Princess of Amber or by the royal title that Akbar bestowed on her, Mariam-us-Zamani—Mariam of her Age.

On August 30, 1569 the Sheikh's prediction came true and a son was born who was named Salim after the Sufi pir. When he became king, Prince Salim took the title of Jahangir and he writes in his memoirs that his father always called him Sheikhu Baba in memory of Salim Chishti. Then to Akbar's amazement the miracle

The birth of Jahangir.

continued and another son Murad was born to a second queen at Sikri in 1570 and a third son at Ajmer in 1572 who was named Daniyal.

The gratitude of a monarch can be a magnificent thing and Akbar was no ordinary king. He was convinced that the blessings of the Sheikh had saved his dynasty. With his heart overflowing with thanksgiving, he also believed that Sikri was an auspicious place. So in spite of having a brand new citadel in Agra, he decided that he would honor Salim Chishti by building a new capital city at Sikri!

Akbar was one of the greatest builders of the Mughal dynasty and Fatehpur Sikri would be the finest creation of his age. The other ambitious Mughal builder would be his grandson Shahjahan who built the Taj Mahal. In 1571 the royal architects, masons and stone carvers moved to Sikri and began work. The material for the buildings was found in the red sandstone of the hill itself. With typical Akbari panache, the top of the hill was sliced off to create the flat area on which a complex of palaces could be built. The city of palaces, pavilions, mosques, open courtyards, gateways and surrounding wells took just fourteen years to build.

Around the main core of the royal palaces and the mosque grew the other buildings—soldier's barracks, stables for horses and elephants, administrative offices, quarters for servants, kitchens, the workshops of craftsmen and the royal mint. The noblemen shifted their residences from Agra and built their mansions on the slope of the hill while the markets and the houses of common people came up at the bottom. It was as if by a wave of his royal wand Akbar made a complete city appeared on the landscape. Then to celebrate his conquest of Gujarat he built the soaring gateway of the Buland Darwaza and renamed his capital Fatehpur Sikri—the City of Victory.

Even today the palaces, the mosque and Salim Chishti's shrine survive in a very good state at Fatehpur Sikri. Wandering through its ghostly corridors one can imagine what it must have been like when it was alive with people. Noblemen in gorgeous clothes walking busily through the courtyards, soldiers standing guard at the gateways, busy officials bent over their low desks writing in big ledgers. Then to shouted orders, the roll of drums and salaaming nobles, Akbar would arrive to give an audience at the Diwan-i-Am, the Hall of Public Audience. He would come and sit on the square throne, resplendent in silks and jewels, lean back against bolsters and listen to the petitions of his subjects gathered below him.

Akbar's wish to be a true Indian king was also reflected in his architecture that evolved into an indigenous style.

All his craftsmen were Indian, many of the stone carvers came from Gujarat and they brought with them typically Hindu motifs like the lotus blossoms, leaves and vines, filigree screens and carved pillars. These were sensitively blended with Islamic geometric and calligraphic patterns to create elegant buildings that visitors admire even today.

The British traveller Ralph Fitch who saw Fatehpur Sikri in 1585 felt it was a greater city than Elizabethan London.

Akbar and his court stayed at Fatehpur Sikri for fourteen years and then in 1585 he left for the Punjab on a long military expedition. Then he visited Kashmir a number of times and only returned to Agra in 1598. Once he was back in the capital Akbar decided to stay at his old citadel, the Agra Fort and not at Fatehpur Sikri. What is surprising is that he never returned to Fatehpur Sikri again. The reason for this has always been a great mystery as none of the chronicles of the time answer the question. Today the red sandstone courtyards lie silent in the sun, the palaces wait for the monarch's footsteps and the gateways no longer see royal processions. The pavilions and mosques only come alive with the arrival of tourists and pilgrims visiting the dargah of Salim Chishti. But as dusk fall and the people leave, the city lies silent once again. Fatehpur Sikri is the most beautiful ghost town in the world.

Historians have speculated about the mystery of Fatehpur Sikri. One theory is that the water supply failed. But it is hard to believe that Akbar's architects while planning the city would have ignored such a basic requirement as water. The city was amply provided with an aquaduct, water tanks and wells, many of them still survive and there was an artificial lake at the bottom of the hill. Travellers visiting the area many years later write about the existence of the lake, though now it is a stretch of fields.

One reason could be that Fatehpur Sikri was an open city and not a fortified citadel and therefore hard to defend. In the latter half of his reign Akbar first faced the rebellion of his half brother Mirza Muhammad Hakim who was being secretly supported by some Uzbeg noblemen in the royal court. Then his eldest son Salim was in a state of sporadic revolt for many years. Akbar may have felt safer in the Agra Fort that held the royal garrison and the imperial treasury.

Those years at Fatehpur Sikri may have been brief but they were the best years of Akbar's reign. It was a time when every aspect of life in the kingdom flourished under the nurturing eye of the king. It was as if nothing escaped the attention of Akbar who had a voracious curiosity about everything. From reforming the administration to building a library, patronizing music. Painting,

Central pillar of 'Hall of Public Audience'.

philosophy and evolving a new religion. Akbar packed in an amazing amount of activities in the middle of all the burdens of running the empire. There was the music of Tansen, the writings of Abul Fazl, the poetry of Faizi and Birbal and the work of the architects, miniature painters. carpet weavers, wood and stone craftsmen all getting the attention of the king, These were the Golden years of Akbar's magnificent reign.

Akbar now got down to the business of consolidating his conquests. It was not an easy task because after the death of Sher Shah Suri the administration had collapsed and the countryside was controlled by local chieftains. First the system of surveying land and the collection of revenue was re-organised. Then new roads and caravan sarais were built and old ones repaired. The irrigation system was improved and farmers were encouraged to increase their farm holdings. He was keen to improve education and financed pathshalas and madrassas. In all this, he was helped by an efficient team of officials led by Raja Todar Mal, whose system of assessing land and collecting revenue was so efficient that it was still in use four centuries later during the British regime.

Akbar also tried to reform some of the social evils prevalent at that time. He banned child marriages, setting the minimum age for marriage at fourteen for girls and sixteen for boys. He abolished the system of *sati*, where a widow was burnt on the funeral pyre with her husband. Akbar is quoted in the Akbarnama saying, 'It is an ancient custom in India for a woman to burn herself on her husband's death, even though she may have been unhappy with him. And give up her priceless life with a cheerful countenance, conceiving it to be a means of her husband's salvation. It is a strange commentary on the magnanimity of men that they should seek their deliverance by means of their wives'. He even persuaded a Bikaner princess not to commit *sati* for the sake of her children.

Panch Mahal, Fatehpur Sikri.

We know so much about Akbar's reign because all the events were recorded in meticulous detail by his historian Abul Fazl. His two mammoth chronicles, the 'Akbarnama' or the History of Akbar and 'Ain-i-Akbari', the Regulations of Akbar are the best source of information on his reign. This was part of Akbar's growing passion for books and keeping records. A magnificent royal library was collected which is said to have over twenty thousand manuscripts. Then he established a department of calligraphers and painters who copied out important manuscripts and then these were illustrated with miniature paintings. Sanskrit works like the Mahabharata were translated at Akbar's orders and he was fond of listening to the stories of the epic, which he called 'Razamnama'—The Tales of the Great War.

Akbar wanted a proper history of the Mughals to be written, so he encouraged members of his family and the court to write down their memoirs. Among them were his aunt Gulbadan and two servants of Hurnayun, Jauhar and Bayazid. The most detailed work was done by Abul Fazl and his books, being official histories are of course full of praise of the king. At the same time another scholar, Badauni was secretly writing his 'Muntakhab-ut Tawarikh'—a bitter, highly critical and jaundiced account that does balance Fazl's worshipful writings. Badauni, a

Buland Darvaza, Fatehpur Sikri.

religious bigot felt slighted by the king's favours to Fazl and seldom found anything about Akbar worth praising.

The years at Fatehpur Sikri were comparitively free from wars and for the first time since he became king, Akbar had the time to indulge his curiosity about religion and philosophy. From his childhood he was fascinated by faqirs, yogis and sufi pirs and loved to listen to readings of the Sufi writings of Hafiz and Rumi. For such an ambitious, hard driving man, there was an odd melancholic side to his character. At times he would withdraw from people to be alone in meditation seeking answers to metaphysical questions about existence and the meaning of life. Badauni writes, that he 'would sit many a morning alone in prayer and meditation, on a large flat stone in a lonely spot'. He was a surprising blend of a mystic and a rationalist and was sincerely religious, believing deeply in god and an earnest seeker of truth.

The greatest influence on Akbar's religious thinking was the liberal philosopher Sheikh Mubarak and his sons Abul Fazl and Faizi. It was an illustrious and scholarly family, Abul Fazl became the royal historian and Faizi the court poet. Sheikh Mubarak was a believer in Sufism that encourages tolerance, love of people and a mystical love of God. He introduced Akbar to the concept of sulh-i-kull—the belief in universal tolerance and peace for everyone. Also Akbar's Hindu wives and friends introduced him to the beliefs and rituals of Hinduism. He began to celebrate the festivals of all religions at his court, from the Hindu Diwali to the Parsi Navroze. He liked to wear his hair long, tied in a knot under a turban in the Rajput style

The Hiren Minar, Fatehpur Sikri.

and at times even wore a tilak on his forehead. He ate very little meat and banned the slaughter of animals on certain days. He was attracted by the Zoroastrain worship of the sun and established a sacred fire in the palace and encouraged Abul Fazl to translate the Christian Gospels into Persian.

In 1575 Akbar built the lbadat Khana, the House of Worship, where once a week he invited priests, thinkers arid philosophers for discussions. In the beginning he only invited Muslim clerics, hoping to listen to wise and learned discussions but the Shia and Sunni priests disappointed the king by their undignified behaviour. They argued fiercely and nearly came to blows over small matters like their seats and order of precedence. Even Badauni writes critically about their unseemly behaviour and how it shocked Akbar. So he widened his invitations and included learned men from every religion—Hindus, Jains, Zoroastrians, Jews, Christians and even the Hindu atheistic school of Nastiks.

In 1579 Akbar sent a request to the Portuguese colony of Goa asking them to send some Christian priests 'with the chief books of the Law and the Gospel'. The Portuguese thinking they had a chance to convert the king to Christianity promptly sent three Jesuit priests to the royal court who, arrived in 1580 led by the Spaniard

Antony Monserrate. He later wrote a detailed account of his stay at the Mughal court, full of fascinating details about life at Fatehpur Sikri and the personality of Akbar.

With great enthusiasm the Jesuits got down to the business of saving the soul of Akbar and his response must have pleased them greatly. He called them the 'Nazarene sages' and listened with great interest to their conversation. He even let Monserrate become the tutor of Prince Murad and did not object when the prince learnt to recite the Christian prayers. The Jesuits were convinced they would succeed in converting the king to their faith. What they did not realise was that Akbar was fascinated by all religions and treated all scholars and priests with the same courtesy and interest.

Krishna's combat with Indra. From the Harivamsa, *a supplement to the Mahabharata dealing with the life of Lord Krishna, was translated into Persian for Emperor Akbar.*

He was a very rare medieval monarch—a naturally curious, truly tolerant person who enjoyed philosophical speculation and went looking for answers in every faith he encountered. As a matter of fact no one was very sure what he believed in. The Muslim Ulema accused him of abandoning his faith and becoming a Hindu. The Hindus were suspicious of the influence of the Jesuits. The Jesuits were nervous of his long conversations with Jain scholars. However, in spite of the accusations of the Muslim clerics, till the end he remained a practicing Muslim. What he did not accept was the unquestioned authority of the Ulema.

So the Jesuits, Ulema and Brahmins were all deeply disappointed when in 1582 Akbar unveiled his new religion, that he called Din-i-Ilahi, or Religion of God. Akbar's new faith was a blend of all that he had heard in the Ibadat Khana and he had taken whatever appealed to him with an even handed generosity. With Din-i-Ilahi Akbar declared himself both the temporal and religious head of the state and he was to be the final arbiter in all religious matters. It was a religion without a priestly class or a holy book and was based on the Sufi idea of the absorption of the soul in the: Divine Being. He then took the place of the head priest at the mosque and read the prayers. The Ulema were outraged when lie stamped his coins with the phrase

'Allahu Akbar' which means God is Great but could also be interpreted as Akbar is God. An interpretation that must have greatly amused a subtle manipulator like Akbar.

Also, as always with a shrewd and pragmatic king like Akbar there was a very practical reason for his unveiling of a new faith. He was trying to find a way to calm the religious unrest that often prevailed in his empire. He realised that the orthodox priesthood of every religion, all battling for power and influence, were the real obstacle to peace in his kingdom. So the simplest way to check their influence was to have a new, religion that he headed as chief priest and preacher.

A small group in the court embraced the new faith but it did not really spread among the people. Akbar never forced the religion on anyone and as the state machinery was never used to propagate the new faith, it remained a tentative elitist faith. Raja Birbal was the only Hindu who accepted the new faith, others like Todar Mal and Man Singh did not. Din-i-Ilahi was a vague synthesis of various beliefs and Akbar's own preference for mysticism and it lacked the simplicity and power of great religions. But it did help Akbar in checking the power of the members of the Muslim orthodoxy who wanted to control the king. Din-i-llahi stayed a personal faith of the king and his friends and never really became a popular religion. It vanished with the death of its founder, Akbar's sons and grandsons preferring to follow Islam.

CHAPTER FOUR

FINAL YEARS

Till the last decade of his life Akbar was often on the move and his conquests continued—first Baluchistan and Kandahar fell and then Kashmir in 1586. With Akbar began the Mughal love affair with the valley of Kashmir and he visited it thrice, even though the hill roads were very difficult. Later his son Jahangir and his queen Nurjahan became passionately fond of the valley and laid down some beautiful gardens with pools and water cascades, like the picturesque Shalimar Bagh in Srinagar.

Once Akbar was back in Agra his eyes turned southward towards the Deccan, an area where the Mughals had not ventured so far. The Deccan was then ruled by five Muslim Sultanates—Ahmednagar, Bijapur, Golconda,

Berar and Khandesh. These Sultanates were prosperous, well established dynasties with a loyal nobility. Also the big distances from Agra to the Deccan must have given them a feeling of security. So when in 1591 Akbar send embassies demanding their submission they did not take things very seriously. The Sultan of Khandesh sent his daughter to be married to Prince Salim, the Bijapur and Golconda rulers politely sent gifts but no one agreed to a formal submission to Akbar. The most powerful of the Daccani rulers, the Sultan of Ahmednagar, Burhan Nizam Shah II treated the imperial embassy with great disdain and did not even bother to respond.

So Akbar decided to move first against Ahmednagar, sending an army led by his son Murad. By the time the imperial army besieged Ahmadnagar, Burhan Nizm Shah had died leaving behind an infant heir and the defence was led by his sister Chand Sultan, who was the regent. The princess defended the fortress with great courage, while calling on her neighbouring kingdoms to come to her aid. Ahmednagar held on till a rescue army from Bijapur and Golconda arrived to attack the Mughals. As an outright victory looked difficult, the Mughals withdrew after Ahmednagar ceded the region of Berar. With Berar, the Mughals acquired their first imperial territory in the Deccan.

Emperor Akbar presiding over the Ibadatkhana.

Once the Mughal army withdrew, the Deccan sultans defiantly re-asserted their independence and stopped sending tribute. There were intermittent battles, wins and losses in the next few years. In 1599, Prince Murad died of alcoholism and was replaced by Akbar's third son Prince Daniyal but the imperial army did not really make any headway. Finally in September 1599, at the age of fifty seven, Akbar himself marched out of Agra at the head of an army of 80,000 men. This was his last important military expedition and he led it with his usual astute courage and vigour, subduing both Ahmednagar and Khandesh. Sadly, none of his sons had inherited his skills at strategic thinking and ability to lead an army.

Akbar's last years were touched by both unrest and tragedy. Some of his greatest nobles and friends had died—his beloved Birbal in 1586, Todar Mal and Bhagwan Das in 1589, Sheikh Mubarak in 1593 and Faizi in 1595. Sadly all his three sons were great disappointments to him and he would see both Murad and Daniyal die of alcoholism. What made things worse was his deteriorating relationship with his surviving son, Salim. Akbar was deeply disappointed with Salim who had become an indolent troublemaker, addicted to alcohol and opium. While he was in the Deccan he had appointed Salim as regent and the prince took the opportunity try and establish his power at court.

When Akbar returned to Agra, Salim marched out against his father and was then forced to withdraw to Allahabad. Here he defiantly had himself crowned as king and had the khutba, the prayer at the mosque, read in his name. Akbar decided to send Abul Fazl to talk some sense into his feckless son but the choice of an emissary was an unfortunate one. Abul Fazl had often been openly critical of Salim and the prince was not pleased. Fazl was on his way to Allahabad when he was attacked and killed by the Bundela Raja of Orchha.

To his dismay Akbar discovered that the Raja had been commissioned by Salim and was generously rewarded for his treachery. A heartbroken Akbar nearly disinherited Salim in favour of his grandson, Salim's eldest son Khusrau. At this juncture the women of the harem stepped in to broker a peace. Akbar's senior wife Salima Sultan Begum travelled to Allahabad and brought back a contrite Salim who fell at Akbar's feet and begged for his father's forgiveness.

Akbar may have forgiven Salim in public but his anger had not abated. Mutamad Khan author of the 'Iqbalnama-i-Jahangiri' writes of the public reconciliation and private punishment, 'The benign Emperor out of affection, drew the Prince in an embrace. The Prince made an offering of a diamond, costing one lakh rupees, nine muhrs of 100 tolas each, two hundred of 50 tolas, four of 25 tolas and three of 20 tolas. He also presented 200 elephants' Then a father's discipline, 'His Majesty signified to the palace attendants to take the Prince to a cell and not to provide him with wine, of which he was an addict. The most severe punishment indeed was for him to be kept away from wine. Immense agony was caused to the Prince and much sorrow had to be borne'.

Then in 1605, when he was sixty three, Akbar fell ill with dysentery and gradually his condition worsened. Aware that he was dying he summoned Salim to his bed chamber and ended the speculation about the inheritance. He put the royal turban on his son's head, handed him his sword and thus anointed him as the heir to the throne. On the night of October 25, 1605 Akbar died and was buried in Sikandra in a mausoleum that he had begun to build, for himself. Salim took the title of Jahangir and ascended the Mughal throne.

Akbar had become king in 1556 and in his magnificent reign of forty nine year he laid the foundation of the empire that would become a legend across the world. It would symbolise a magnificent opulence and add the word 'mogul' to the English language. Travellers carried back tales of a royal court with its fabulous palaces and ornate pageantry, astounding displays of treasures and majestic processions of caparisoned elephants and prancing horses. Later Mughul kings led even more glamorous lives, Akbar's grandson, the sybarite Shahjahan would sit on the jewel encrusted Peacock Throne and wear the diamond Kohinoor. But it was Akbar who began it all.

Akbar in his old age.

Even after centuries, the character of Akbar comes remarkably alive through the many chronicles of the period. Behind the gorgeous portraits and legendary exploits what was this man called Akbar really like?

Like all great men he was a fascinating mix of the ordinary and the remarkable. This was a man who became king at thirteen, survived many challenges to the throne, built an immense empire and ruled as unquestioned monarch for nearly fifty years. These are achievements that needed some very special qualities of head and heart.

He was a true leader of men who inspired absolute loyalty. As a warrior he fought with a reckless courage, often putting his life in danger. As a general, he always led his men into battle and was a shrewd and ruthless military strategist who never lost a battle. He was a tough energetic man, who enjoyed taking physical risks—riding wild elephants, taming horses and facing tigers during the hunt. A large part of his life was of course spent going to war, which meant arduous expeditions in all kinds of weather, through rough terrain and then the stress and danger of battle.

Gateway to Akbar's tomb, Sikandra.

Akbar was a very organised and hard working king and his daily work schedule would have exhausted most men. He slept very little at night and ate just one meal a day. The rest of the time was spent in the work of the empire. As his son Jahangir recollects, 'His nights were passed in wakefulness; and in the day too he slept very little, so that the total period of sleep in night-and-day did not exceed four-and-a-half hours. He treated wakefulness at night as something gained out of the given lifetime'. As a matter of fact, in spite of their image as luxury loving oriental potentates, as the Mughal kings worked very hard. Among the most meticulous and conscientious were Akbar and later his great grandson Aurangzeb.

Abul Fazl's detailed records give us a pretty good idea of a day in Akbar's life. It began with the public audience at the Diwan-i-Am to listen to petitions and pass judgments. Then moving to the Diwan-i-Khas for private audiences, he received ambassadors, listened to reports from the provinces and took decisions on state matters. On some days he inspected the royal horses and elephants, on others he visited the karkhanas, the royal workshops. After lunch he relaxed for awhile and then went back to work, with his assistants reading out reports and important papers. In the evenings there maybe some entertainment like music or dancing, animal fights and games. Akbar employed spies, stationed all across the kingdom and he personally heard their reports at night and then just before going to bed he always listened to readings from books.

Akbar was inherently a humane and just man who made sure he was easily accessible to people. At the same time he was an absolute monarch who expected unquestioned obedience from everyone and if defied he could be fearful in his anger. He took pride in being just and there are only a few examples, like his sacking of the Chittor Fort, when he behaved with any unnatural cruelty. For a medieval monarch he was remarkably free from prejudices. For the first time in India, a Muslim king welcomed Hindus into the inner circle of friends and advisers.

In the Ibadat Khana, where he gathered the scholars of the land, he was probably the only person who was genuinely free of religious prejudice. He was most influenced by liberal thinkers like the Sufis Sheikh Mubarak and Sheikh Tajuddin and by the Zoroastrian scholar Mahyarji Rana. He was trying to delink religion from the state and that was a remarkable effort in medieval times. Like most of his actions his religious policy too was based more on reason and pragmatic reality than on any passionately held beliefs. He wanted peace in the kingdom and he wanted to be the supreme authority. For Akbar the empire and the dynasty always came first.

The persecution of Hindus went down drastically during his reign. Taxes like jizia and a pilgrimage tax were abolished and temples were once again built without the fear of destruction. Raja Man Singh built magnificent temples and ghats at Varanasi and on a visit there Akbar not only toured the temples he also went to see the ruins of Buddhist monasteries at nearby Sarnath. He banned the enslavement of prisoners and freed all his slaves. He appointed a man belonging to the untouchable chandal caste as the head of his own palace guard and gave him the title of Khidmat Rai and one of his miniature painters, Daswant, was the son of a poor palki bearer.

It was the humane, open mind of this benign despot that made him a 'genius for gaining the love and loyalty of people'. He transformed himself from being the leader of a minority ruling elite to being a popular king of Hindustan. Within a few years of his reign Indians felt he was their very own monarch and not an alien leading a military occupation. He laid the foundation of a truly Indian monarchy and in 1857, when north India rose against the British it was in the name of the Mughals.

Akbar sincerely believed that the welfare of his subjects was his responsibility. So he tried to stop the practice of sati, banned child marriages and tried to check the sale of liquor. He ordered equal inheritance rights for Muslim women and discouraged the taking of many wives. Of course he himself had a large harem! He encouraged Todar Mal to create a revenue system that controlled the exploitation of the farmers by landlords. When Prince Murad was appointed the governor of Malwa, Akbar wrote to him of the responsibilities of a ruler, 'Let not differences of religion interfere with policy, and be not violent in inflicting retribution. Adorn the confidential council with men who know their work. If apologies be made, accept them.'

He was a voraciously curious man and there was a hunger to know and understand everything from the way a palace was built to how a carpet was woven. Monserrate writes, 'the king is considered by some to be mad, because he is very dextrous in all jobs, because I have seen him making ribbons like a lace maker, and filing, sawing, and working very hard. (He watches, even practices) for the sake of amusement, the craft of an ordinary artisan'.

His greatest fascination was with spiritual matters, a surprising side of a man who seemed to be such an earthy, pragmatic and ambitious personality. He needed time to think and meditate, 'a rationalist and a dreamer, a mystic and a seeker after truth; he covered under his inexhaustible energy a soul melancholy'. Nearly illiterate he loved books, built up an immense library and got books in Sanskrit and Persian translated. He listened to poetry, history, theology and philosophy and among his favourite bed time reading was his grandfather's memoirs, the 'Baburnama' and the Persian translation of the Mahabharata.

Our image of the gorgeous court of the Mughals with its rigid etiquette and a cultured courtly style was something Akbar created. He knew how important it was to impress people by pomp and pageantry and he enjoyed the theatre of playing the magnificent monarch. He would sit in a court filled with rich furnishings, wearing jewels and silks, the nobles gathered before him clad in brilliant clothes waiting upon their resplendent monarch. Then there was the elaborate bowing and presenting of precious gifts and dramatic rituals with loud announcements, the beating of drums and blowing of trumpets. He created this super human, semi divine monarch, encouraging rituals like the sijda, where subjects greeted him by prostrating themselves on the floor. He gave the empire its character, its traditions and values. What came to be known as the 'Mughalia' culture was often a product of Akbar's fertile mind.

In spite of the fact that the women in the harem were hidden behind the purdah, they were educated and influential at court. Akbar's queens like Ruquayya Begum and Salima Sultan Begum kept a close eye on the working of the empire. One of Akbar's closest advisers was his mother, the formidable Hamida Banu who was consulted on important matters. The women attended court, sitting behind a curtain and were known to call out with their own requests to the king. When Akbar and Salim were estranged it was the harem women who engineered reconciliation. Some were scholars like his aunt Gulbadan who wrote her autobiography. Others were good businesswomen, owning ships and land. In

Later reigns Nurjahan the wife of Salim would rule in her husband's name. Mumtaz Mahal, Shahjahan's wife held the royal seals and his daughter Jahanara, a poet and thinker also managed the port of Surat and was one of the richest women in the empire.

Akbar's court was a glittering gathering of brilliant personalities. He was said to have the navaratnas, the nine jewels in it. He made sure the best talents in art and culture belonged to his court. He sent a polite request, one that could not be refused, to the Raja of Rewa for his court singer. In this way the legendary Mian Tansen arrived at Fatehpur Sakri. Then Baz Bahadur the ruler of Malwa, who had lost his kingdom to Akbar, joined the court. He was a greater singer than a king and became one of the leading musicians. Painters like Basawan, Mukund and Daswant, received the personal attention and encouragement of Akbar. He introduced the art of knotting Persian carpets into India and the dhurrie weavers at Fatehpur Sikri today are the remnants of those karkhanas. He even led the fashion, creating new styles in clothes and is described by Monserrate as wearing an elegant silk and zari dhoti.

Finally, Akbar as remembered by Jahangir in his memoirs, 'Tuzuk-i-Jahangiri', 'Although he was illiterate, so much became clear to him through constant intercourse with the learned and wise, that from his conversations with them, no one could take him to be illiterate. And he was so well acquainted with the niceties of verse and prose compositions that such deficiency could not be imagined'

'In his august personal appearance he was of middle height, but inclining to be tall; he was of wheatish complexion, his eyes and eyebrows were black and his features were more refined than (merely) handsome, he was slender waisted with a broad chest, and his hands and arms were long. On the left side of his nose he had a fleshy mole, very agreeable in appearance, of the size of half a common pea. Those skilled in the science of physiognomy considered this mole a sign of great prosperity and exceeding good fortune. His august voice was very resonant and in speech and discourse was very well modulated. In his actions and movements he was not like the people of this world, and the light of God emanated from him.'

CHRONOLOGY

HEADLINES OF AKBAR

1542, 15th October

Born at Umarkot, eldest child of Humayun and Hamida Bano.

Grandson of Babur. Named Jalaluddin Mohammad Akbar.

1555

Humayun restored to the throne of Delhi.

1556, January

Humayun dies after a fall from library steps.

1556, 14th February

Akbar is king, the third of the Mughal dynasty.

1556, 5th November

Second Battle of Panipat.

1560

Bairam Khan dismissed as regent.

1562

Akbar marries daughter of Raja Bharmal of Amber.

1564

Repeals Jizya tax on Hindus.

1565

Builds fortress at Agra.

1568, February

Siege and fall of Chittor.

1569, 30th August

Birth of eldest son Salim.

1570, 7th June

Birth of second son Murad.

1571

Building of Fatehpur Sikri begins.

1572, 10th September

Birth of third son, Daniyal.

1572, November

Conquest of Gujarat.

1573

Raja Todar Mal develops new revenue system.

1575

Ibadat Khana, the house of worship built at Fatehpur Sikri.

1576, 21st June

Battle of Haldighati. Rana Pmtap defeated.

1576, July

Conquest of Bengal.

1580

Jesuit mission arrives from Goa led by Father Monserrate.

1581

Half brother Mirza Muhammad Hakim, ruler of Kabul, rebels.

1582

Inaugurates his new religion of Din-i-Ilahi.

1586, February

Death of friend and adviser, Raja Birbal.

1589, 6th May

Death of court singer Mian Tansen.

1591
Prince Salim tries to seize power and fails.

1599, 11th March
Death of Prince Murad.

1599, September
Leads his last expedition to the Deccan.

1600, 23rd July
Salim tries unsuccessfully to seize Agra.

1602
Salim declares himself king at Allahabad.

1602, August
Abul Fazi killed by the Raja of Orchha.

1604, April
Death of Prince Daniyal.

1605, 25th October
Death of Akbar at the age of sixty three, after a reign of forty nine years.
Buried at Sikandra.

1605
Prince Salim ascends the throne as Nuruddin Jahangir.

BIBLIOGRAPHY

THE MUGHAL EMPIRE—Bharatiya Vidya Bhawan

THE MUGHAL EMPIRE—John F. Richards

GREAT MUGHALS—Abraham Eraly

THE WONDER THAT WAS INDIA—S.A.A. Rizvi

THE GREAT MUGHALS—Bamber Gascoine

EPISODES IN THE LIFE OF AKBAR—Shireen Moosvi

AKBAR & HIS INDIA—Irfan Habib.

PAINTINGS FROM THE AKBARNAMA—Geeti Sen

AIN-I-AKBARI—Abul Fazl

AKBARNAMA—Abul Fazl

Akbar conquered Chittor but the spirit of Mewar could not be crushed. Udai Singh died in 1572 and was succeeded by his son Rana Pratap. Akbar tried once again to build an alliance with him. He sent three missions, one led by Todar Mal but the defiant Pratap refused to bow to the might of the Mughals. War was inevitable and the two armies met at Haldighati on 18th June 1576 and even though the Rajputs fought with fierce courage their army was too small compared to the Mughal might. Pratap was wounded but managed to retreat into the hills where he could not be followed. Helped by tribal Bhil warriors, he continued to wage a guerilla war from the hills of Mewar. Over the years he regained much of his kingdom and he never bowed to the Mughals.

By the time Akbar was in his mid twenties, he had conquered most of North India and some of the southern kingdoms had become his allies. There was peace in his kingdom and the Mughal treasury overflowed with gold and jewels. Within the first ten years of his reign he had become a supreme monarch. Now Akbar the empire builder began to transform himself into Akbar the king.

CHAPTER THREE

THE KING

In 1568, Akbar was twenty six and the monarch of an Indian Empire. His kingdom covered most of north India from Kabul in the west to Bengal in the east and most of the rulers of neighbouring kingdoms acknowledged his sovereignty. There was peace in his kingdom and few dared to rise in rebellion against him. Trade was growing and the royal treasury was also filling up nicely with tribute and revenue. In spite of it all, Akbar had little peace as he had no son who could inherit this kingdom. For a diehard imperialist like him this was a devastating disappointment.

In spite of a harem filled with queens and concubines, none of Akbar's male children had survived. He was a worried man and being deeply religious he now turned